BEAST
HANK McCOY

MARVEL GIRL
JEAN GREY

CYCLOPS
SCOTT SUMMERS

ANGEL
WARREN WORTHINGTON III

ICEMAN
BOBBY DRAKE

HERE TO STAY

BRIAN MICHAEL
BENDIS
WRITER

DAVID
MARQUEZ
ARTIST, #6-8

STUART
IMMONEN
PENCILER, #9-10

WADE VON
GRAWBADGER
INKER, #9-10

MARTE
GRACIA
**WITH RAIN BEREDO (#9-10)
COLORISTS**

VC'S CORY
PETIT
LETTERER

COVER ART: STUART IMMONEN, WADE VON GRAWBADGER & MARTE GRACIA

JORDAN D.
WHITE
ASSISTANT EDITOR

NICK
LOWE
EDITOR

COLLECTION EDITOR: **JENNIFER GRÜNWALD**
ASSISTANT EDITORS: **ALEX STARBUCK** & **NELSON RIBEIRO**
EDITOR, SPECIAL PROJECTS: **MARK D. BEAZLEY**
SENIOR EDITOR, SPECIAL PROJECTS: **JEFF YOUNGQUIST**
SVP OF PRINT & DIGITAL PUBLISHING SALES: **DAVID GABRIEL**
BOOK DESIGNER: **RODOLFO MURAGUCHI**

EDITOR IN CHIEF: **AXEL ALONSO**
CHIEF CREATIVE OFFICER: **JOE QUESADA**
PUBLISHER: **DAN BUCKLEY**
EXECUTIVE PRODUCER: **ALAN FINE**

ALL-NEW X-MEN VOL. 2: HERE TO STAY. Contains material originally published in magazine form as ALL-NEW X-MEN #6-10. First printing 2013. ISBN# 978-0-7851-6821-8. Published by MARVEL WORLDWIDE, INC., a subsidiary of MARVEL ENTERTAINMENT, LLC. OFFICE OF PUBLICATION: 135 West 50th Street, New York, NY 10020. Copyright © 2013 Marvel Characters, Inc. All rights reserved. All characters featured in this issue and the distinctive names and likenesses thereof, and all related indicia are trademarks of Marvel Characters, Inc. No similarity between any of the names, characters, persons, and/or institutions in this magazine with those of any living or dead person or institution is intended, and any such similarity which may exist is purely coincidental. **Printed in the U.S.A.** ALAN FINE, EVP - Office of the President, Marvel Worldwide, Inc. and EVP & CMO Marvel Characters B.V.; DAN BUCKLEY, Publisher & President - Print, Animation & Digital Divisions; JOE QUESADA, Chief Creative Officer; TOM BREVOORT, SVP of Publishing; DAVID BOGART, SVP of Operations & Procurement, Publishing; C.B. CEBULSKI, SVP of Creator & Content Development; DAVID GABRIEL, SVP of Print & Digital Publishing Sales; JIM O'KEEFE, VP of Operations & Logistics; DAN CARR, Executive Director of Publishing Technology; SUSAN CRESPI, Editorial Operations Manager; ALEX MORALES, Publishing Operations Manager; STAN LEE, Chairman Emeritus. For information regarding advertising in Marvel Comics or on Marvel.com, please contact Niza Disla, Director of Marvel Partnerships, at ndisla@marvel.com. For Marvel subscription inquiries, please call 800-217-9158. **Manufactured between** 4/1/2013 and 5/13/2013 by R.R. DONNELLEY, INC., SALEM, VA, USA.

10 9 8 7 6 5 4 3 2 1

Born with genetic mutations that gave them abilities beyond those of normal humans, mutants are the next stage in evolution. As such, they are feared and hated by humanity. A group of mutants known as the X-Men fight for peaceful coexistence between mutants and humankind. But not all mutants see peaceful coextistence as a reality.

ALL·NEW X·MEN

The Beast used a time machine to bring the original five X-Men (Cyclops, Marvel Girl, Iceman, Beast and Angel) to the present.

He hoped their presence would convince the adult Cyclops — who killed Professor Xavier while posessed by a cosmic force and is now leading a revolutionary team alongside Magneto — to change his ways.

The original X-Men are shocked to find a world that is the opposite of the one Xavier had envisioned. The young Jean Grey called a vote and her team decided to stay until they can make Xavier's dream a reality.

6

SO, I SEE YOU DID SOME REDECORATING.

SORRY.

IT'S OKAY.

NO, IT'S NOT. I'M--

IT'S NOT LIKE I CLEAN.

HONESTLY, IF I HADN'T HEARD IT, I PROBABLY WOULDN'T HAVE NOTICED.

YOU WERE NICE ENOUGH TO LEND ME YOUR ROOM.

I'M SORRY.

YOU'VE BEEN ASLEEP FOR A WHILE.

GUESS I NEEDED IT.

WHAT--I'M SORRY--WHAT IS YOUR NAME AGAIN?

I'M KITTY PRYDE.

KITTY PRYDE.

I WAS THE HEADMISTRESS OF THE SCHOOL.

BUT AS LONG AS YOU AND THE ORIGINAL X-MEN ARE GOING TO STAY HERE... I'LL BE WORKING WITH YOU.

I'VE NEVER-- I HAVE NEVER HAD A DREAM LIKE THAT BEFORE.

WELL, YOU'RE HAVING A LOT OF FIRSTS THIS WEEK.

YOUR TELEPATHIC POWERS CAME INTO BLOOM--

YOU'RE LIVING IN A DIFFERENT TIME THAN YOU'RE SUPPOSED TO BE.

SNIFF...

WHERE ARE THE OTHERS?

DON'T WORRY ABOUT THEM RIGHT NOW.

THEY'RE FINE.

IT'S A FUNNY THING--

YESTERDAY I WAS THE LEADER OF THE X-MEN...

THAT WAS *YESTERDAY*.

AT LEAST TO ME.

IF YOU'LL EXCUSE ME.

HOW?

HOW COULD I *BE* THIS THING?

HOW COULD I HAVE *DONE* THIS?

AND I READ ONLINE LAST NIGHT THAT REED RICHARDS THINKS THAT--THAT THE SPACE-TIME CONTINUUM IS A LIVING THING, YOU KNOW.

LIKE A PERSON, AND IF WE'RE USING IT AS A TOY TO--

SHUT IT, BOBBY.

WRRROOOOOMMM

SON OF A--!!!

!

?

?!

YOU DID.

WOW.

WERE WE FRIENDS?

YOU WERE THE CLASS IN FRONT OF ME.

BUT YES, YEAH, I ADMIRED YOU.

KIND OF.

KIND OF?

OH MAN. SORRY.

SORRY.

YOU WERE A LITTLE TOUGH ON ME.

SOMETIMES.

MY NAME IS STORM.

SCOTT IS NOT GOING TO HAVE EVERYONE'S TRUST HERE.

THEY ARE GOING TO NEED YOU.

AND YOU'RE STORM?

YES.

ARE WE FRIENDS?

VERY GOOD FRIENDS.

I THOUGHT SO.

YOU CAN LOOK IN MY HEAD JUST THIS ONCE BUT AFTER THAT...

WAIT. WHERE IS SCOTT?

I DON'T THINK HE'S HERE.

HE LEFT.

WOLVERINE WENT AFTER HIM.

WELL...

%#$@!!

EXCUSE ME, DO YOU HAVE A MAP?

A MAP?

A MAP OF THE UNITED STATES? OR THE WORLD?

DOESN'T YOUR PHONE HAVE A MAP?

MY PHONE?

UH, YEAH!

WHY IS ALL THE WATER IN BOTTLES?

BECAUSE IT'S BOTTLED WATER.

WHY IS THE WATER BOTTLED NOW?

AS OPPOSED TO WHEN?

DID SOMETHING HAPPEN TO THE WATER?

ARE YOU GOING TO BUY SOMETHING OR--WOW!

YOU KNOW WHO YOU LOOK LIKE?

YOU LOOK JUST LIKE HIM!

YOU LOOK LIKE THAT GUY WITH THE-- WITH THE--

YOU LOOK *JUST* LIKE HIM!

HOW MUCH IS THIS? I'LL TAKE IT.

$4.99. ARE YOU GUYS RELATED OR--?

FIVE DOLLARS?! FOR A *MAGAZINE?!* PLUS TAX.

THIS PLACE *IS* A NIGHTMARE.

HOW DO YOU EXPECT ME TO--?

WHAT DO YOU CARE, TONY STARK?

WHY DOES HE HAVE THIS MUCH MONEY IN HIS POCKET?

BECAUSE IT'S NONE OF YOUR DAMN BUSINESS.

WHERE THE HELL DO YOU THINK YOU'RE GOING?

I HAVE TO SEE FOR MYSELF.

I HAVE TO SEE WHAT I HAVE BECOME.

NO ONE SEEMS TO HAVE THE COURAGE TO TELL ME TO MY--AAAAAND THERE GOES CYCLOPS.

SURE, LEAVE ME HERE, SCOTTIE.

I DON'T WANT TO BE HERE IN THE FIRST PLACE AND NOW YOU LEAVE ME HERE.

YOU GUYS STICK ME HERE AND YOU DON'T EVEN--

HUH-- OKAY.

WHAT IS--?

AM I NUTS OR DID THE GROUND JUST BURP?

WHAT HAS HAPPENED TO THE SCHOOL? WHAT HAS HAPPENED TO THE--?

WELL, THIS IS... UNEXPECTED.

OH MY GOD...

SO...
WHAT ARE
YOU, ME FROM
THE PAST?

YES.

YES?

UH...THE
ENTIRE ORIGINAL X-MEN
TEAM WAS BROUGHT HERE
TO THE FUTURE--UH, TO THE
PRESENT--TO HELP DEAL WITH
WHAT'S GOING ON WITH
SCOTT SUMMERS...

THE ORIGINAL
X-MEN ARE HERE
RIGHT NOW?

YES.

JEAN GREY?
JEAN GREY IS
HERE?

YES.

WHO
DID THIS?
BEAST?

YES,
ACTUALLY.

UH, WHERE
DID YOU GET
THOSE...
ARE THOSE
METAL?

7

MANHATTAN,
NEW YORK.

People

The Avengers
Mutant Cover
Up?

NEW
MUTANT
??

CAN I HELP YOU?

I NEED HELP WITH ONE OF THE SAFETY DEPOSIT BOXES.

SURE. DID YOU BRING YOUR KEYS?

I DIDN'T, ACTUALLY.

DO YOU HAVE TWO FORMS OF IDENTIFICATION?

WELL, SORT OF. I'M SURE WE CAN--

AGH!

OH... THAT'S BETTER.

THANK YOU, SCOTT SUMMERS.

The Honor of Your Presence Is Requested

WHAT IS GOING ON WITH YOU, ALL OF A SUDDEN?

YOU HAVE NO IDEA WHO IS IN THERE RIGHT NOW...

WHO IS IN WHERE?

THE SAFE DEPOSIT BOX ROOM.

WHO?

CYCLOPS IS IN THE BANK?

YES!

CYCLOPS FROM THE CRAZY X-MEN?

I AM GOING TO *EXPLODE.* LITERALLY EXPLODE.

HE'S-- HONEY, HE'S WANTED BY THE POLICE.

NO. COME ON.

THAT'S JUST THE--THE-- THE CONSPIRACY AGAINST MUTANT--

GUARD!

HEY JERRY!

WE--WE CALLED THE POLICE!

YOU DON'T PULL A GUN ON SOMEONE JUST BECAUSE THEY'RE *DIFFERENT* THAN YOU.

YOU CAN'T *PULL A GUN* ON SOMEONE FOR *WALKING INTO A BANK.*

HE DIDN'T *ROB* THE BANK.

DID YOU ROB THE BANK?

NO.

I'M NOT *GOING* WITH YOU!

LET ME DO WHAT I WANT TO DO!!

YOU'RE WELCOME.

LEAVE ME *ALONE!!*

ARE YOU HUNGRY?

SEE, *HE* DIDN'T ROB THE BANK.

SO HERE'S THE DEAL: WE ARE LEAVING.

IF YOU *SHOOT* ME, IT WON'T HURT *ME* AND I WILL CUT OFF YOUR HANDS.

I'LL GO BACK TO WHEREVER I CAME FROM AND YOU WON'T HAVE *HANDS.*

SCOTT, DARLING, NOT EVERYTHING IS WHAT IT SEEMS TO BE.

WHAT DOES THAT MEAN?

C'MERE.

LET *GO* OF ME!!

JUST--

I NEEDED SOMEONE YOU WOULD BELIEVE AND SOMEONE THEY WOULD BE AFRAID OF...

HE WAS MY ONLY CHOICE, REALLY...

HANK McCOY BROUGHT YOU TO THE HERE AND NOW?

THAT MAN IS A CONUNDRUM.

THIS IS *PUNISHMENT*.

HE SAYS HE BROUGHT US HERE TO STOP THE COMING MUTANT CIVIL WAR, THE GENOCIDE, AS HE PUT IT.

HE'S A LIAR. HE BROUGHT US HERE TO PUNISH ME.

HE'S MAD ABOUT XAVIER.

IT MIGHT BE BOTH THINGS.

HANK IS A SON OF A BITCH FOR BRINGING ME HERE.

MAYBE.

BUT HE *IS* RIGHT.

THINGS HAVE NEVER BEEN MORE CHAOTIC FOR OUR PEOPLE.

AND YOU, THE OTHER YOU, IS A *BIG* REASON WHY.

I *HAVE* TO BE DOING ALL OF THIS FOR A *REASON*.

I *HAVE* TO TRULY BELIEVE THAT THIS IS FOR THE BEST INTEREST OF OUR PEOPLE.

IT'S NICE TALKING TO THE YOUNG YOU.

UNCOMPROMISING. IDEALISTIC.

THE OTHER YOU? NOT SO MUCH. NOT ANYMORE.

YOU'RE NOT MAD AT ME FOR KILLING CHARLES XAVIER?

YOU DIDN'T KILL CHARLES XAVIER. THE OLDER YOU DID.

MAYBE.

MAYBE?

THE WORD IS HE WAS UNDER THE INFLUENCE OF A POWER HE COULDN'T CONTROL.

SCOTT SUMMERS WOULD *NEVER* KILL CHARLES XAVIER. RIGHT?

I *NEED* TO TALK TO HIM.

(WHICH IS A WEIRD THING TO SAY.)

IT'S A WEIRD THING TO HEAR.

AND YOU SHOULD.

AND, IN MY OPINION, HANK IS RIGHT.

YOU SHOULD PROBABLY SH.. HIM DOWN BEF.. HE HURTS HIMS.. OR OTHERS.

I GUESS HANK IS THINKING THAT MAYBE YOU HATE YOURSELF ENOUGH TO STOP THIS BEFORE IT GETS *MORE* OUT OF CONTROL.

WHO ARE *YOU* IN ALL THIS?

YOUR SCHOOL'S BEEN TAKEN OVER BY THAT MONGREL WOLVERINE SO HE CAN TEACH ALL THOSE LITTLE MUTANTS TO BECOME FERAL KILLING MACHINES.

THAT WAS *NOT* CHARLES XAVIER'S DREAM.

THAT WAS NOT WHAT YOU FOUGHT FOR.

AND LOST FOR.

WAIT! WHERE'RE YOU GOING?

WOLVERINE HAS TRACKED YOU. HE'S ON HIS WAY HERE.

TRACKED ME?

HE'S A TRACKER.

YOU MIGHT WANT TO, THIS IS A GOOD TIP ACTUALLY, YOU MIGHT WANT TO START CARRYING AROUND A NOTEBOOK OF WHAT EVERYBODY DOES.

KEEP TRACK OF MUTANTS AND WHAT THEY DO. FOR STRATEGY, YEAH?

IT WAS VERY GOOD TO MEET YOU LIKE THIS.

I WAS ALWAYS A *BIG FAN* OF THE OLD YOU.

HOW CAN I FIND YOU?

YOU DON'T NEED TO FIND ME.

YOU NEED TO FIND YOURSELF.

ON NUMEROUS LEVELS.

DID YOU TRY TO ROB A BANK?

WHY HAVEN'T YOU KILLED ME YET?

I JUST MET YOU.

NO.

I MEAN ME--THE *ADULT* ME.

CLEARLY YOU COULD.

YOU'VE MADE IT VERY CLEAR YOU WANT TO.

YUP.

AND I COULD KILL *YOU* RIGHT NOW.

AND IF I DO MY MATH RIGHT THAT MEANS YOU'D CEASE TO EXIST. BOTH OF YOU.

EXACTLY. YOUR PROBLEM'S SOLVED.

MAYBE I'VE LIVED LONG ENOUGH TO KNOW THAT KILLING IS THE EASIEST THING.

SAVING SOMEONE IS A LOT DAMN HARDER.

MAYBE IT WAS CHARLES XAVIER WHO TAUGHT ME THAT.

GET IN.

YOU'RE WASTING MY DAY.

WHAT IF I CAN'T BE SAVED?

STEAL MY #$@& EVER AGAIN I CUT SOMETHING OFF.

NICE.

TRAINING TIME.

I'M KITTY PRYDE, YOUR NEW INSTRUCTOR.

LET'S GET FIFTY PUSH-UPS IN TO WARM UP.

WARM UP?!!

FIFTY PUSH-UPS IS THE WARM UP?!

WHERE'S WARREN AND SCOTT?

THEY'LL GET THEIRS.

TELL YOU WHAT, HOT SHOT.

YOU TAKE A SWING AT ME, RIGHT HERE, NO POWERS... CONNECT ONE.

AND I'LL NEVER BUG YOU WITH TRAINING AGAIN.

I'M NOT HITTING A GIRL.

I'M NOT A GIRL, I'M A FIERCE COMPETITOR, YOU SEXIST TWIT.

DON'T CALL ME A--

I KNEW HANK HERE WAS THE SMART ONE... I DIDN'T REALIZE YOU WERE ACTUALLY THE DUMB ONE.

DON'T. LISTEN, HEY. DON'T CALL ME--

DROP AND GIVE ME FIFTY OR SHOW ME YOU CAN FIGHT LIKE A MAN, ICE BOY.

DON'T CALL ME--

ICE WAAAGGH!

AND THAT'S WHY YOU NEED TRAINING.

FROM NOW ON I EXPECT YOUR COMPLETE COOPERATION OR YOU'RE BENCHED.

YOU'RE SHHO MEAN.

LOOK WHO'S BACK.

AND--?

TWO HOUR DRIVE. HE SAID NOTHING. YOU'RE IN CHARGE OF THIS FROM NOW ON. I'M DONE.

THANK YOU FOR NOT KILLING HIM.

WHATEVER FAVOR I OWED YOU, WE'RE EVEN.

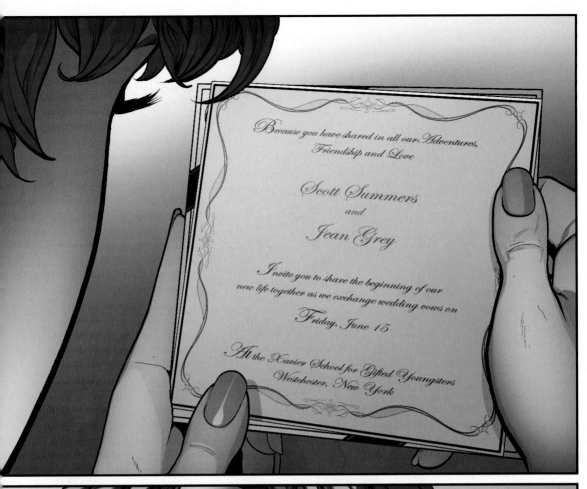

Because you have shared in all our Adventures, Friendship and Love

Scott Summers
and
Jean Grey

Invite you to share the beginning of our new life together as we exchange wedding vows on

Friday, June 15

At the Xavier School for Gifted Youngsters
Westchester, New York

8

ISN'T THIS THE BEST?

SOMETIMES YOU TAKE FOR GRANTED ALL THOSE NORMAL EVERYDAY PEOPLE *STUCK* DOWN THERE, IN TRAFFIC, JUST SITTING THERE AND--

WHY?!

WHOA!

WHY WON'T YOU TELL ME WHAT HAS *HAPPENED* TO YOU?

WHOA! YOU NEED TO *RELAX.* YOU NEED TO--

STOP.

MAN, WAS WARREN ALWAYS LIKE THIS? YOU'RE LIKE A--A COILED SPRING.

WHY DID YOU JUST REFER TO ME AS WARREN?

YOU'RE WARREN *TOO.*

WELL, HUH, SEE, THIS IS GOING TO BE HARD FOR YOU.

WARREN WAS--I MEAN WE WERE *BORN* WARREN BUT WE *ARE...*ANGEL.

I'M ANGEL.

WE--WE'RE ANGEL.

NO...

TWO OF THEM AND A **HUNDRED** OF YOU!

(I HAVE TO START SCREENING BETTER.)

TWO ANGELS.

SO MUCH FOR GETTING INTO HEAVEN.

AND IF I FIND OUT THAT YOU KNOW--

HELLO, CAPTAIN. I'VE BEEN STUDYING UP ON RECENT EVENTS.

I REALIZE THAT YOU AND I HAVE FOUND OURSELVES ON DIFFERENT SIDES OF THE FENCE ON A LOT OF ISSUES.

I JUST WANTED YOU TO KNOW THAT I PLAN ON DOING EVERYTHING I CAN TO MAKE IT RIGHT.

I HOPE YOU GIVE ME THE CHANCE.

NICELY DONE.

YOU'RE WELCOME.

PLEASE TELL ME YOU HAVE THIS UNDER CONTROL.

I DON'T HAVE ANY OF IT UNDER CONTROL.

AT LEAST TRY TO KEEP ME IN THE LOOP.

THERE IS NO LOOP.

JUST--

I'LL DO MY BEST, CAPTAIN.

THAT'S ALL I CAN ASK.

THAT'S ALL I CAN DO.

NO!!! YOU-- YOU MADE AN AGREEMENT!

I WAS OUTVOTED!

I'M GOING HOME. I DON'T *LIKE* IT HERE.

WE-WE-WE SHOULDN'T BE SEEING THIS STUFF.

DUDE, LET'S TALK ABOUT IT. WE'LL--

HAVE YOU *SEEN* ME?

HAVE YOU SEEN WHAT I'VE *BECOME*?

SOMETHING REALLY BAD HAPPENED TO ME.

I DON'T *WANT TO* BE HERE.

IF YOU GO BACK, CHARLES XAVIER WILL KNOW WHAT WE HAVE DONE HERE.

GOOD.

THEN WE GO BACK TO OUR TIME, AND CHARLES WILL ERASE OUR MEMORIES, AND WE WILL--

I DON'T *CARE!*

STOP TALKING IN *CIRCLES.*

IF THIS IS THE WAY OUR LIVES GO IT'S BECAUSE WE *EARNED* IT!

I WANT TO GO HOME.

I WANT TO GO HOME AND THE SECOND I CAN GO HOME I'M GETTING THE HELL *AWAY* FROM YOU PEOPLE!

YOU--YOU WANTED TO TEACH ME SOMETHING...YOU WANTED TO *SHOW* ME SOMETHING?

YOU SHOWED ME THAT I NEED TO *GET THE HELL AWAY* FROM--!!

IS HE HAVING A STROKE?

WARREN?

WHAT'S FOR LUNCH?

IS ANYBODY ELSE *STARVING?* I'M STARVING.

UM...

UH...

HE'LL BE FINE.

WE'RE NOT GOING BACK.

JEANNIE? DID YOU JUST--?

HE'LL BE FINE.

YOU'RE NOT ALLOWED TO GO DIGGING INTO OTHER PEOPLE'S MINDS AND JUST *CHANGE* THEM FOR YOUR OWN REASON.

HENRY, DON'T *YOU* OF ALL PEOPLE START *LECTURING* ME ON USING YOUR GOD-GIVEN THINGS FOR SELFISH PURPOSES.

WE'RE STAYING.

IT WAS DECIDED.

HE JUST NEEDS TO CALM DOWN.

SO I HELPED HIM CALM DOWN.

EVERYTHING IS FINE.

9

I TRIED TO **SAVE** YOU.

THAT'S RIGHT.

I WAS BEING SARCASTIC.

BY TRYING TO SAVE ME YOU CLEARLY SHOWED THAT YOU **DON'T KNOW** THAT MY MUTANT POWER IS **PHASING.**

I BECOME **INTANGIBLE** AT WILL.

IF YOU HAD **DONE** YOUR RESEARCH YOU WOULD ALSO KNOW THAT IF I PHASE THROUGH ELECTRONICS I CAN DISRUPT THEIR CIRCUITRY AND **SHUT THEM DOWN.**

THEY **CAN'T** HURT ME.

(WAS THERE READING I WAS SUPPOSED TO DO?)

I WAS THE ONLY PERSON YOU **SHOULDN'T** HAVE BEEN SAVING.

EVERYBODY ELSE IN THE VICINITY INCLUDING YOUR TEAMMATES WAS IN SERIOUS JEOPARDY.

HANK? WHAT DO YOU THINK **YOU** DID--?

POINT TAKEN. NO NEED TO BELABOR IT.

CYCLOPS, YOU ARE VERY GOOD IN THE FIELD.

BUT YOUR MEN WERE **NOT** LISTENING TO YOU.

YOU LOST CONTROL OF THE SITUATION BEFORE THE SITUATION HAD EVER BEGUN.

ARE THEY MY MEN?

YOU WERE THE ONE BARKING ORDERS.

YOU, ALL OF YOU, HAVE TO DECIDE WHO IS **LEADING** THE TEAM.

EACH OF YOU WILL BE GETTING A COPY OF THE TRAINING FOOTAGE.

I SUGGEST YOU RELIVE THE PAIN AND WE WILL DISCUSS MORE OF IT AFTER DINNER.

THAT SOUNDS **AWESOME.**

WHAT DOES THIS HAVE TO DO WITH **ANYTHING?**

WHAT THE HELL IS THIS?

HOLD YOUR FIRE. I THINK THAT'S-- MARIA HILL.

WHAT IS SHE *DOING* HERE?

POP INSPECTION.

I HATE HER.

AR

AT EASE, AGENTS OF S.H.I.E.L.D. I BRING YOU VICTOR CREED, A.K.A. SABRETOOTH.

WE JUST CAUGHT HIM TRYING TO BREAK INTO THE LATVERIAN EMBASSY AND THIS WAS THE CLOSEST SUPER-HIGH SECURITY FACILITY AND I DON'T WANT TO TAKE ANY CHANCES.

NO ONE TOLD US YOU WERE COMING, MA'AM. I DIDN'T KNOW I WAS.

IT'S OKAY--THOSE ARE STARK TECH PURE ADAMANTIUM SHACKLES FROM TONY STARK'S PERSONAL COLLECTION, DON'T YOU KNOW.

FIND A HOLE AND THRO HIM IN IT

WHERE SHOULD WE PUT HIM?

HE DOESN'T SMELL GOOD.

THEY RARELY EVER DO.

HE WAS TRYING TO BREAK INTO AN EMBASSY?

HEY, YOU KNOW WHAT... I TOTALLY FORGOT.

THOSE AREN'T ADAMANTIUM SHACKLES.

DO WE EVEN *HAVE* ADAMANTIUM SHACKLES?

WE EITHER FIGHT CYCLOPS, TAKE HIM HEAD ON...

...OR WE JOIN HIM IN HIS FIGHT WITH THE HUMANS.

I DON'T WANT TO DO EITHER.

NO ONE IN THE SCHOOL WANTS TO.

BUT IF EVERYTHING IS *SO BAD* WITH THE HUMANS, WHAT WILL IT TAKE FOR YOU TO *PUSH BACK?*

WHEN THE HUMANS SHOW UP AT OUR FRONT DOOR WITH A TANK AND A GIANT MUTANT-HUNTING SENTINEL.

OR WORSE...

MICROSCOPIC MUTANT-HUNTING SENTINELS...AND TELL US THAT'S ENOUGH...

THEN I WILL FIGHT.

BUT THE ONLY THING I CAN THINK OF THAT WILL MAKE THE HUMANS SHOW UP ON OUR DOORSTEP WITH A TANK AND MUTANT-HUNTING ROBOTS IS THE MOST POPULAR MUTANT IN THE WORLD STANDING IN FRONT OF CAMERAS AND *PICKING A FIGHT.*

YES.

I BROUGHT YOU HERE TO *WAKE HIM UP.*

I DESPERATELY WANT SCOTT SUMMERS TO *SNAP OUT OF IT.*

YOU'RE WONDERING WHERE THE MUTANT GENOCIDE IS?

I'M TELLING YOU THAT IF I, WE, PLAYED THIS RIGHT... WE'VE AVOIDED IT.

I DIDN'T BRING YOU HERE TO *WITNESS* THE MUTANT GENOCIDE.

I BROUGHT YOU HERE TO *AVOID...*

...A MUTANT...

...GENOCIDE.

OH MY STARS AND GARTERS.

SCOTT, *STOP!!*

WHAT?

MYSTIQUE?

YOU BUMP INTO A CHARACTER LIKE MYSTIQUE...YOU *TELL* SOMEONE.

I DON'T *HAVE TO.*

NOT WITH YOU HAVING *JEAN* POKE AROUND IN MY BRAIN WHENEVER THE HELL YOU WANT.

HOW DID MYSTIQUE EVEN KNOW YOU WERE...

YOU'LL HAVE TO--

WHAT?

SON OF A--

MORNIN'.

NOT IF YOU PUT MONEY ON THE PACKERS.

NOW WHO TOLD YOU TO DO THAT?

HOW'S THE WIFE?

RECOVERING.

HOW MANY MORE KIDS ARE YOU GONNA HAVE?

BUDDY, THE BABY STORE IS CLOSED.

WHAT'S WITH ALL THE EXTRA SECURITY?

BIG TRANSFER TODAY.

18 MILLION?

KEEP IT DOWN.

I'VE NEVER HANDLED ANYTHING OVER A COUPLE OF MILLION.

HEY, WE GET PAID THE SAME EITHER-- OH MY GOD!

LOCKDOWN!! WE ARE IN LOCKDOWN!!

GOD IN--!!

HOLY--!

COME ON, WOLVERINE! YOU HAVE TO GIVE HIM PROPS FOR HAVING GALACTUS-SIZED COHONES.

SHUT UP.

BACK TO YOUR SEATS.

DO WE GET TO WATCH THE FIGHT? IS THERE EXTRA CREDIT IF WE--

I'M NOT HERE TO FIGHT.

WE'RE NOT HERE TO FIGHT ANYONE.

ESPECIALLY NOT FELLOW MUTANTS.

WE ARE HERE TO CLEAR THE AIR AS BEST I CAN AND MAKE YOU AN OFFER.

JEAN GREY SCHOOL FOR HIGHER LEARNING. WESTCHESTER, NEW YORK.

SCOTT SUMMERS, YOU ARE OUT OF YOUR MIND.

IT'S HARD NOT TO TAKE THAT PERSONALLY, PROF. KITTY.

I MEANT THAT ONE OVER THERE.

I KNOW, BUT STILL...

AND MY OFFER IS THIS...

FSHHAM

AGH!

I CAN'T BELIEVE THAT HAPPENED *AGAIN*.

THIS TIME I KILL IT.

X-MEN, I CAME HERE FOR A REASON.

SLIM...IT'S ALMOST WORTH *NOT* KILLING YOU WHEN I HAD THE CHANCE TO WATCH THINGS LIKE *THAT* HAPPEN...

BUT YOU NEED TO @#$@# THE @#$@#$ OFF.

NOT UNTIL I HAVE SAID WHAT I CAME HERE TO SAY.

NO ONE WANTS TO HEAR YOU TALK YOURSELF OUT OF TAKING RESPONSIBILITY FOR THE @#$@ YOU'VE DONE IN YOUR LIFE.

GUT HIM, TEACH.

SHUT UP.

WHAT DO YOU WANT?

EVERYONE HERE HAS A CHOICE.

STAY HERE AND KNOW THAT WE, AS YOUR FELLOW MUTANTS, WILL PROTECT THIS SCHOOL FROM ALL COMERS.

WITH EVERYTHING WE HAVE.

WE DON'T WANT YOUR--

BUT THE NEW XAVIER SCHOOL IS WHERE YOU WILL TRAIN TO FIGHT AND FIGHT BACK *HARD*.

WE TRIED BEING MESSENGERS...

WE TRIED BEING PACIFISTS...

WE TRIED HIDING IN PLAIN SIGHT.

WE TRIED EVERYTHING BUT LETTING THEM KNOW WHAT WE REALLY TRULY ARE.

WHAT XAVIER TRAINED US TO BE...

WHAT IS *THAT*, SCOTT?

WARRIORS.

WHO WILL DO *ANYTHING* FOR WHAT WE BELIEVE IS RIGHT.

AND AREN'T YOU THE POSTER BOY FOR THAT, HENRY?

REALLY?

YOU'RE *NOT*?

YOU DO WHATEVER *YOU* THINK IS RIGHT.

NO MATTER WHAT THE COST TO SPACE OR TIME NO MATTER WHAT THE COST TO OUR FUTURE OR PAST.

WE *ARE* FIGHTERS.

SINCE WE WERE KIDS... WE FIGHT WITH *EVERYTHING* WE HAVE.

AND I SAY WE REMEMBER THAT AND WE TAKE THIS *HUGE* SECOND CHANCE OUR PEOPLE HAVE BEEN GIVEN AND WE *FIGHT* FOR OUR RIGHT FOR *ALL* OF US TO LIVE IN THIS WORLD BECAUSE IF WE DON'T...

WHO WILL?

DAMMIT! AT EASE, AGENTS OF S.H.I.E.L.D....

ON YOUR KNEES! HANDS ON YOUR HEAD!

I AM ACTING S.H.I.E.L.D. *DIRECTOR MARIA HILL!*

YOU CALLED ME HERE!

GRAB HER WEAPONS!!

I SAID: AT EASE!

SCANNING.

SHE READS CLEAN.

SORRY, DIRECTOR.

SHOW ME WHAT HAPPENED HERE.

SHE--SHE CAME IN HERE WITH VICTOR CREED... SABRETOOTH.

SHE LOOKED JUST LIKE--JUST LIKE YOU...

DAMN.

I COULDN'T READ THEIR MINDS.

MAGNETO'S HELMET LETS HIM DODGE A PSYCHIC ATTACK, JEAN.

FROM WAY BACK IN HIS BROTHERHOOD OF EVIL MUTANTS DAYS.

HE PROBABLY HAS THE ENTIRE TEAM OUTFITTED WITH TECH TO DODGE YOU AFTER YOUR *LAST* ENCOUNTER.

DAMN, WE COULD'A HAD THEIR BASE OF OPERATIONS.

JUST LIKE THAT.

THEY'RE PROBABLY HIDING ON UTOPIA SOMEWHERE.

IT'S THE FIRST PLACE WE'D LOOK.

HE'S AT THE LAST PLACE WE'D LOOK.

OR MAYBE THE LAST PLACE WE'D LOOK IS THE FIRST PLACE HE THINKS WE'D LOOK.

SHUTTING UP NOW.

I MUST SAY: SCOTT SUMMERS SEEMS GENUINELY AS DISAPPOINTED IN ALL OF YOU AS YOU ARE WITH HIM.

I NOTICED THAT TOO.

DO YOU THINK ANY OF YOUR STUDENTS WILL GO WITH HIM?

ALL-NEW X-MEN #6 X-MEN 50ᵀᴴ ANNIVERSARY VARIANT
BY CHRIS BACHALO & TIM TOWNSEND

ALL-NEW X-MEN #7 X-MEN 50TH ANNIVERSARY VARIANT
BY NICK BRADSHAW & JASON KEITH

ALL-NEW X-MEN #8 X-MEN 50TH ANNIVERSARY VARIANT
BY STUART IMMONEN, WADE VON GRAWBADGER & MARTE GRACIA

ALL-NEW X-MEN #10 MANY ARMORS OF IRON MAN VARIANT
BY GREG HORN

I thought it might be interesting, as part of the "behind the scenes" material, to give readers a look into the editorial and review process of a few pages that underwent some changes before the final image. Marvel Comics are by nature very collaborative, and the input made by editors and writers regarding the art is incredibly important. So...

#6, PAGE 5, PANEL 1

This page was an awesome opportunity to draw the huge cast of the Jean Grey School. To take some of the edge off an already very complex page and panel, I leaned pretty heavily on one of my favorite tools for digital art creation: SketchUp. It's a great tool that allows a user to intuitively build 3D models that I use extensively in my workflow.

For this scene, I created a model of the cafeteria, added some brick texture to the walls and started populating the tables with all the colorful characters from the school.

HUGE kudos go to editors Nick and Jordan for providing me with an official school roster to make sure didn't mess it up!

#6, PAGE 3

This was a tricky page since it's important to keep the gore level low in a Marvel comic, while still portraying the ferocity and viciousness Wolverine is capable of. In the first version of this panel, I drew Jean after being slashed so I wouldn't have to explicitly show the wound she received, but editors Nick and Jordan, as well as Brian, all made the excellent point that we really should be able to see her face and reaction to sell the moment.

In version two — which ended up being the final version — we got to see her face, with her hair and shoulder hiding the worst of the damage, while showing the claws popping out behind her head give the sense of just how terrible Wolverine's strike was.

My original layout for this panel was meant to evoke WW2-era propaganda posters, with Madam Hydra against a backdrop of Hydra exoskeletons flying in formation. The rest of the team was afraid that the extreme low angle would obscure her face too much, so in the revised sketch I inched the "camera" up just enough so we could still see her, while also giving us the sense of power that low-angle shots offer.

An unexpected consequence of changing the angle, though, was that we wouldn't be looking quite so directly up into the sky, and so I dropped in the building behind her to give a sense of scale and verticality.

#8, PAGE 16

This was an incredibly fun page to draw. Brian has a such a gift for writing hilarious dialogue, and the relationship between Kitty and Bobby is so fun to play with. This was a case, though, where my initial layout, while visually functional, really didn't take into account leaving enough space for all the dialogue.

The collaborative nature of comics — between writer and artist, and also between words and pictures — can be seen right on the page. Tall panels can, among many other things, give dialogue room to breathe.

The last page of the issue — and the last page of my three-issue run on *All-New X-Men* — and such a huge moment for Jean. We really needed to get this page right. There was a lot of back-and-forth discussion between Nick, Jordan, Brian and myself about how to sell the moment that Jean takes charge, and possibly begins down a very dark path. There were two really important things to show here: Jean's imposing presence, and the stunned — and horrified — reaction of her teammates.

As you can see from all the sketches, most of initial drawings were really focused on Jean, without showing much of the other X-Men.

In the final version of the page, we drastically increased Jean's size, letting her dominate the page while also giving us a clear look at of all the X-Men, and how each of them reacts differently to what this person they love so much has said and done, and what it might mean for all of their futures.

THE FREE *MARVEL AUGMENTED REALITY APP* ENHANCES AND CHANGES THE WAY YOU EXPERIENCE COMICS!

To access the Marvel Augmented Reality App..

- Download the app for free via **marvel.com/ARapp**
- Launch the app on your camera-enabled Apple iOS® or Android™ device*
- Hold your mobile device's camera over any cover or panel with the **AR** graphic.
- Sit back and see the future of comics in action!

*Available on most camera-enabled Apple iOS® and Android™ devices. Content subject to change and availability.

ALL-NEW X-MEN AR INDEX